RESTORATIVE JUSTICE

The Journey of Healing

Joe Barnett

Illustrated & Designed by Edwin Sexton

I am truly grateful, blessed, and downright humbled by the support of family, friends, and strangers that I experienced writing this book.

I dedicate this book to all of the survivors of crime. Godspeed to us all. We are not victims, but we survived what has not killed us

The best fighter is never angry

LAO TZU

Table of Contents

CHAPTER 1
Introduction

Most of the population have been fortunate enough to not have experienced a violent crime in which they were the victim. The news today is full of stories about ordinary citizens that have fallen victim to a violent crime in one way or another. However, the chances of the offender being brought to justice and being held accountable for their actions is a small ratio, especially if the crime is minor. Why would anyone not want to report a crime against their person or property? Shame? Guilt? It takes too much time and effort on the part of the victim in proportion to the crime? All of these answers are correct.

We are living in a digital age, an age of instant gratification, where we can have just about anything we want at any time we want it. This has created a void of patients and has taught us that there is no need to process our feelings. Negative feelings are passé, and we deserve what we want, no matter what the cost as long as the monthly payment will fit into our budget.

The criminal justice system is slow to change in the digital age. There is no instant gratification for the plaintiff or defendant. The over-burdened court system is rife with petty misdemeanors ranging from possession charges to theft. Most of the accused accept a plea deal in lieu of a jury trial. Many defendants would rather "get it over with" than to fight the wrongful charge. Defendants often feel they have no choice but to plead guilty for various reasons. Some of those reasons include the cost it would take to hire a reasonable attorney, the time that would be consumed by going to court repeatedly, missing work, and adding to an already stressful situation. A defendant who accepts a wrongful conviction is not what we are going to discuss. The topic of this book is restorative justice, which is a tool to help the victim and offender both heal. A long journey down a narrow path is where the story of restorative justice begins.

The goal of this text is not to reduce the number of crimes, whether petty or otherwise, in the United States, but to bring awareness to an underused process in the criminal justice system that can help restore victims' rights in an attempt to make their life whole again. The caveat is that it will not work in every situation, and it is by no means a miracle cure. You will always have those feelings of how a crime made you feel. We may forget what people say, but we never forget how they made us feel. Learning to live with those feelings is a process not many can achieve. The good news is there is help available and that is a process we know today as restorative justice, and I hope it will make a difference in your life.

CHAPTER 2

Justice? What Justice?

One fateful night in 1995, a young mother, Sharletta Evans, who lived just outside of Denver, Colorado, drove to an apartment complex to pick up her great-niece. The night before, there had been a drive-by shooting at the apartment complex where her great-niece resided. Startled, Evans wanted to take her great-niece out of that situation and have her stay in, what she viewed as, a safer location. The events that were about to unfold that night would change Sharletta's life forever.

Sharletta's plans consisted of picking up her great-niece and taking her to spend a few nights at Sharletta's apartment until the violence quelled. Sharletta drove to the apartment complex where her great-niece resided to pick her up. The exchange should have been quick. So quick in fact that when Sharletta ran into the apartment complex, she had her two-small sons in the car with the engine still running. In just that short period of time, shots were heard outside the apartment building. It was another drive-by shooting.

Once the shooting stopped, Sharletta returned to her car, only to find that one of her son's had been fatally shot in the head during the drive-by shooting while she was inside the apartment complex trying to rescue her great-niece from the fear of a drive-by shooting.

Fortunately for Sharletta, and the rest of the community, three teens were arrested and charged with the drive-by shooting that killed Sharletta's son (Simpson, 2016). It was later determined that one of the teens, Raymond Johnson, who was involved in the drive-by shooting, fired the fatal shot that struck Sharletta's son, Casson, in the head.

Justice may have been served when Johnson was sentenced to life *with* parole, according to the criminal justice system; but in what capacity was justice served? One could argue that justice was served based on the laws of the land and that Johnson had a fair and impartial trial and was rightfully convicted. This conviction will close the file on the case, according to the courts, but what about those close to the case that are left to pick up the pieces? There is some closure to be had for the family, and the rest involved after a conviction, however, there are many questions that need to be answered at the intersection of the end of the trial and the healing process.

CHAPTER 3

Goals & Degrees of Restorative Justice

According to the Restorative Justice Consortium, restorative justice has a main focus of restoring the victim, or community, rather than punishing the offender with a harsh prison sentence. There is also an element of the offender taking responsibility and acknowledging the wrong that they have done and encourages the offender to make reparations to the victim and the community in hopes of making them whole again.

Another goal of restorative justice is to, ideally, prevent the offender from repeating their actions on another victim in the future (Restorative Justice, nd). This is done by bringing the victim and offender together and allowing the victim to describe to the offender how they were affected by the crime. In contrast, the offender will have the chance to let the victim know the motivating factor that led them to commit the crime against the victim. After the offender is released from confinement, the hope is they will remember the words of the victim and think twice before committing a crime against another person.

Similar types of restorative justice practices have been practiced for centuries in the Asian, Celtic, Hebrew, and Arab cultures. In those cultures, the goal of restorative justice has been to regularize indigenous practices as well as peacemaking between divided societies. However, in the modern context, restorative justice was believed to first be used in 1974 when a probation officer arranged for two teenagers, who had been on a vandalism spree, to meet with their victims to discuss and agree on restitution for the victims.

Restorative justice has been known by many names. When the practice of restorative justice became popular, most practitioners referred to it as a victim-offender reconciliation program, victim-offender mediation and victim-offender dialogue as it spread across North America in the 1980's and 1990's (Umbreit & Greenwood, 2000). While the name of restorative justice was going through changes, so was the concept of what encompassed the practice.

In restorative justice, there are typically three main stakeholders. The number one stakeholder is the victim, followed by the offender and then lastly the community of care in which the crime took place (Ortiz, 2019).

The goal of restorative justice, in this situation, is to obtain reparations for the victim, have the offender acknowledge responsibility, and to achieve reconciliation for the community.

Types and degrees of restorative justice practice is shown in the following graph. The three main stakeholders are represented by the circles and show the varying degrees of restoration brought on by the restorative justice process.

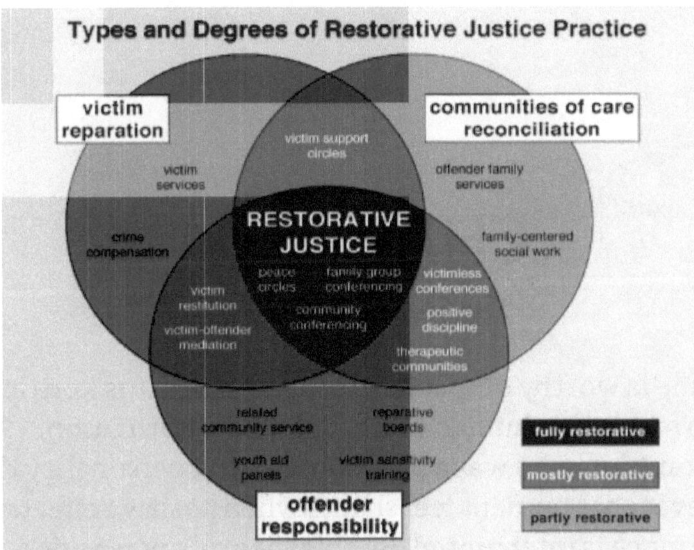

Figure 1: Restorative Justice Typology

When the practice of restorative justice only represents one group of primary stakeholders, the process is known as only partly restorative. If the practice involves two primary stakeholders, but eliminates a third, it is known best as mostly restorative justice. It is only when all three stakeholders are actively involved that restorative justice has served the purpose for which it was intended (Rogers & Miller, 2018).

Defining the word "restorative," can be complex and viewed differently based on past, cultural, and lived experiences. Since no two people have the same view, a "Compass of Shame" was created by psychiatrist Donald Nathanson to explain the psychology and feelings of all humans who have been victim of a crime.

CHAPTER 4
The Compass of Shame

Shame is worthy of special attention since it is a critical factor in regulating human social behavior (Nathanson, 1997). Silvan Tomkins, who was a psychologist and personality theorist, believes that humans feel shame when positive effects from an experience is interrupted. By this theory, a person does not need to do anything wrong in order to feel shame. An interruption of enjoyment or excitement is replaced with shame. This helps us to understand why victims will typically, at one point or another, feel a sense of shame, even though they did not commit the crime and do not deserve to bear this burden.

The Compass of Shame Nathanson developed helps us to understand the different ways humans react to the feeling of shame.

As outlined in the following diagram, the compass focuses on four main points of emotions that are felt by the victim. Nathanson noted that while most victims "complete" the compass of shame, there are many victims who stop at one point or another. The victim can stay at a specific point for years or even a lifetime. It has been suggested that working with a therapist to move through the points of the compass is useful to overcome the feeling of shame and guilt felt by the victim, but another tool that can be used is restorative justice. Not every victim is the same and talk therapy may not work for one as it does the other. Restorative justice has a proven track record of working to help the victim recover when all other approaches have failed (Kirkwood & Hamad, 2019).

Figure 2: The Compass of Shame (adapted from Nathanson, 1992)

Typically, those with a positive self-esteem will quickly move past the feeling of shame. However, it is important to note that one of the four poles, "attack other," is a direct response for the violence that we see today. Many times, a victim of a crime will lash out physically or verbally against others which is a direct correlation to the feeling of shame. This lashing out, or turning the tables, often represents the feeling of entitlement one has after they are victims of a crime. By nature, the act of restorative justice will allow the victim to access a platform where shame, guilt, and other emotions are acknowledged. When these feelings are expressed, it will reduce their intensity and take away the power that shame has introduced (McCold & Watchtel, 2003).

Defining restoration through the use of fair practice requires some creative thinking. As mentioned previously, what is fair is in the eye of the beholder. Kim and Mauborgne (2003) have broken down the use of fair practice into three principals: engagement, explanation and expectation clarity.

The act of engagement involves listening to individuals, taking their opinion into account, and involving them in the restoration process. While their opinion may seem irrational, it is an important part of conflict resolution that helps us to know the stake in which each party claims in this process. At this point, the individual who is involved in the active listening of both sides becomes a quasi-mediator of conflict resolution (Ellison & Partridge, 2012).

As a mediator, once you know the opinions and feelings of each party, it is important to come to a non-biased resolution based on the information that you have heard up until this point. Once you have reviewed all of the information, you need to back up your opinion with an explanation whether good or bad. As stated earlier, what is fair is in the eye of the beholder. One party may see your explanation as irrational while the other is comfortable with the decision that was made.

Finally, the expectation of clarity should be made visible to all involved. This expectation should be made known for situations now and in the future. In order to be completely transparent, the clarity of the conversation and decision should be 100% understood (Amjad & Riaz, 2019).

The idea of fair process represents the way in which a leader will exert their authority. This can be seen in many different situations such as managers and even parents. The philosophy behind fair process is that when those in authoritarian positions can help others make a positive change by helping others as equals rather than doing things for them (Schiff, 2018).

As part of the social discipline window, fair process relates to how leaders utilize their authority in different professions and various roles. Authoritarian roles include teachers, parents, managers, and in some cultures, elderly people (Kumar, Karabenick, S. A., Warnke, J. H., Hany, & Seay, 2019).

The leading hypothesis of restorative justice is that people want to be happy and lead fulfilling meaningful lives. However, sometimes, a person may be put in a negative situation and chooses actions that do not manifest pro-social changes, which snowballs until a crime is eventually committed. Restorative justice can help to change the thinking of some to a more positive outlook for both the offender and the victim (Johnstone, 2020).

CHAPTER 5

Circles
More Than Just Shapes

A circle, in the human psyche, is more than just a shape, rather it is a symbol of equality (Bohmert, Duwe & Hipple, 2018). Take for instance the tale of King Arthur of Camelot and the Knights of the Roundtable. The table in which the knights sat was not rectangular, but circular, to show that all who were there are equal and trustworthy. A rectangular table would be considered a nonverbal cue that whomever sat at the head of the table is the most powerful in the group and looked upon as such.

The history of the word "circle" is often attributed to the Greeks (Wilson, 2018). Although many ancient civilizations existed who were familiar with the symbol based on ancient drawings of the moon and sun, but no name was ever attributed to this object. The Greeks were the first to invent the word "Kirkos" or "Kuklos," which loosely translates into English as "hoop" or "ring." In more modern industrial times, the circle is accredited for the invention of the wheel and wheels. On the mathematical side of things, the circle has been shown to be a key factor in Geometry and Calculus.

So why is a circle associated with the practices of restorative justice? In this situation, a circle can be used to proactively build relationships and community (Buchanan, 2019). In part, circles give people the opportunity to listen and speak to one another in an atmosphere that is safe, much like in the time of King Richard of Camelot and the Knights of the Roundtable.

When people are placed in a circle, it gives them the opportunity to tell their stories and offer their own perspectives without judgment and ridicule (Igwe, 2018). All are equal in a circle. While in a circle, it gives the opportunity and chance for all to experience conflict resolution, decision making, healing, and a chance to exchange information that may not have been known otherwise. Unlike the rectangular table, circles offer safety from one-sided arguments and hierarchy positioning.

Figure 3: District Attorney

The concept of the circular roundtable can be used in any virtual setting. As children, we are conditioned by sitting in circles at school for games and other learning activities. This type of activity continued on into middle school and was used to promote creativity later in high school and then to include productivity in the workplace. It wasn't until 1992 that Yukon Circuit Court Judge Barry Stewart introduced the "sentencing circle," in which he involved members of the community, in which a crime had occurred, on the appropriate sentencing for the accused offender (Percival, 2003).

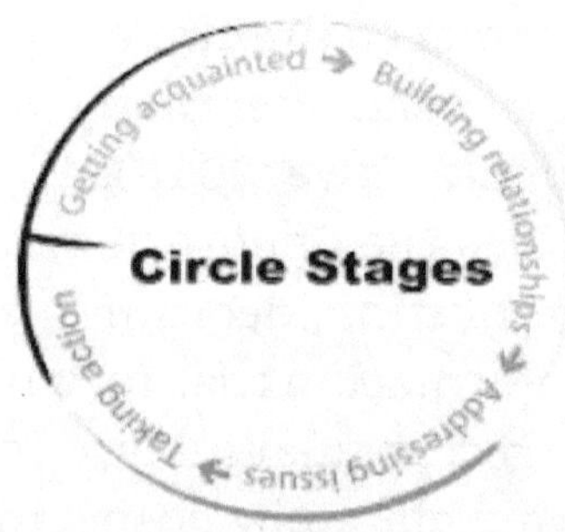

Figure 4: How to Run a Meeting Like a Restorative Justice Talking Circle

The use of circles in restorative justice must be done in an orderly fashion with rules and consequences. Circles must have structure which is often achieved in a sequential format. In a circle, participants are only allowed to speak one at a time, while moving in a clockwise direction until the circle is complete and everyone has spoken (Elliott, 2018). If the circle is broken, meaning a participant has spoken out of order, the sequence continues, but the outspoken participant is bypassed until the next revolution.

Many criminal justice professionals who use restorative justice as a technique for healing often use what is referred to as a talking piece (Winters & America, 2014). The circle and talking piece can be found in throughout history and in ancient civilizations. When a person is holding the talking piece, they are known as the circle keeper.

The psychology behind the talking piece is that it will fill the void of those who feel marginalized to have an equal voice which results in respectful communication. In order for the talking piece to work efficiently, it should relate to the participants in the circle in a personal manner. A talking piece for a circle of grieving construction workers could be a fallen co-worker's hard hat, or something else personal to the participants that can tighten the bond of the circle. Choosing a talking piece that is meaningful to the circle translates into trustworthiness and equality (Mehl-Madrona & Mainguy, 2014). While the talking piece may not have any intrinsic value, the symbol for which it holds is priceless.

Figure 5: Talking Piece

If, as a facilitator of a circle, you do not have a talking piece that is of any sentimental value to the participants, it is important to create a value – or worth – to an object that the circle can relate to in the discussion. It is up to you to find a common denominator that would resonate with the circle in which they could take ownership of the talking piece. The talking piece would then have a meaning and can be respected by other within the group.

The circle is governed by topics that are raised by the facilitator and strict adherence is mandatory to the chosen topics. This will eliminate the "back-and-forth" rhetoric that often leads to misunderstandings and counter-productive measures. The talking piece will help to eliminate this type of miscommunication within the circle (Talking Piece, nd). Notably, the talking piece will also give those individuals within the circle who are normally silenced by others to have a fair chance to express their opinion. Those within the circle that may disagree with the speaker at the time, must be patient, and wait their turn to express their feelings on the topic.

It is possible for a circle to not have a leader or facilitator. This type of circle is called a non-sequential circle. The idea behind a non-sequential circle is one that is similar to a panel the openly discusses ideas and resolutions. Since there is no facilitator, it is the responsibility of the circle to maintain order and stay on track. One person can be designated as a note taker, which has a dual responsibility of keeping the circle on topic and taking notes that may be relevant to the topic being discussed (McCold, 2001).

Another useful circle is often referred to as the "fishbowl." In this approach, an inner circle of participants discusses a problem that will need a solution. The inner circle will follow the rules of the sequential circle where one person speaks, and the direction of conversation is maintained in an orderly format (Hung, 2015). Inside this inner circle, there should be an empty chair. This chair represents more than an empty seat, it represents an outside perspective.

Outside of the inner circle should be other assigned circles which have the ability to watch the inner circle discuss problems and resolutions. The empty chair in the inner circle will allow those outside the inner circle, who have been observing the conversation, to join the inner circle, relay their idea, and then return to a circle outside of the inner circle.

There is no magic ingredient that will make circles or restorative justice work correctly. It is a mere art than it is an actual science. Circles work best with some groups, while other groups are not so open and forthcoming with information. There is no real reason why this happens. Some would say it is the body chemistry of the group or the non-verbal communication that each participant exhibits. While these are good theories, there is no actual data that tells us why this happens. I often compare it to predicting the weather. We know it could possibly rain, there is a greater chance in this city, and we know it could start raining about 1 p.m. If we can hit the trifecta, then we know there is a greater chance of restorative justice working.

CHAPTER 6
Informal Restorative Justice Techniques

Restorative justice can be used in both formal and informal settings. The formal setting is highly structured, which is most of what I have described up until this point. However, restorative justice can be used in some unlikely places that we think of as an informal setting.

The most common, informal setting in which restorative justice is used is in the school and classroom setting. You may not think of a classroom as an informal setting for restorative justice techniques, but they are used frequently and have become quite popular in the past decade.

To use restorative justice techniques effectively as an informal tool, you must present affective statements as well as employing affective questioning (McCold & Watchtel, 2001). We can think of affective statements as a form of communication that relays how a person is feeling. Affective questioning is letting the other party know how their behavior has affected a single person or others as a group.

Applying these techniques to an informal setting, such as a classroom, is a valuable tool that a teacher will be able to use as a teachable moment for the entire class. As an example, if a class is taking a test, and one student disrupts the whole class, this is where informal restorative justice will be used as a learning experience. The teacher should let the disruptive student know how they make her feel when they disrupt the class. These feelings can range from sadness to anger based upon the severity of the disruption. The teacher should then follow up with an affective question such as "who were you trying to disrupt," "how do you think it made them feel?" Instead of being automatically punished by the teacher, the disruptive student has the chance to communicate about their disruptive behavior and think about what they have done and how their actions affected more than one person.

When you ask affective questions geared toward the disruptive student's behavior, and bring in the other students that were affected, you have created an informal restorative justice circle.

Informal restorative justice techniques can virtually eliminate the need for more lengthy restoration practices. Constant use of informal restorative justice techniques creates an environment that empathy, awareness, and personal responsibility. Many professionals argue that informal restorative justice techniques are more effective at achieving social discipline than punishing a wrongdoer (Akinyemi, 2018).

CHAPTER 7

"I Accepted Him as My Son"

Drawing on previous chapters, we have learned that circled are more than just shapes. Circles can be symbols of peace, transition, and continuity, which brings me to my next point.

What happened in the case of Sharletta and the murder of her infant son? Sharletta completed the restorative justice program that the city of Denver, Colorado, District Attorney had offered to help restore some of what she had lost.

Meeting with the murderer of your child is not something that everyone would be capable of doing, but Sharletta did and it transformed her life. Sharletta sought out the meeting with the killer, Raymond Johnson, so she could get closure to her unanswered questions from the night of the murder.

During the course of the meeting between the two, Sharletta made a big decision: she forgave Johnson. When questioned, Sharletta said that she forgave him because it was the only way she could move on with her life and be there for her surviving son. Sharletta explained that Johnson clutched his chest and wept. It was in this moment that Sharletta hugged Johnson and accepted him as her son.

Johnson's parents and family were absent from his presence during the trial and later as he was serving his prison sentence. The response from Johnson moved Sharletta to step in and be the parent that Johnson never had growing up, even while he served life in prison.

The meeting between the two, and the subsequent outcome, is the goal of restorative justice. Making peace with the circumstances in life, whether large or small, and opening up to forgiveness of someone who has done you harm. As the victim, it is important for you to understand the choices and decisions the offender had to make, and was given, to get to the point where you were wronged. It is that understanding that will make you aware that you could be one bad decision away from being given the same choices and making similar decisions like the offender that is incarcerated for the crime against you.

References:

Akinyemi, G. O. (2018). Restorative Justice: A Critical Review. *EC Psychology and Psychiatry, 7*, 862-868.

Amjad, S., & Riaz, N. (2019). The concept and scope of restorative justice system: Explaining history and development of the system for the immediate need of society. *International Journal of Law, September.*

Bohmert, M. N., Duwe, G., & Hipple, N. K. (2018). Evaluating restorative justice circles of support and accountability: can social support overcome structural barriers?. *International journal of offender therapy and comparative criminology*, *62*(3), 739-758.

Buchanan, A. G. (2019). Seventeen years of restorative justice circles: The Yellow Medicine County experience. *Contemporary Justice Review*, 1-18.

District Attorney. (n.d.). Retrieved April 18, 2020, from https://www.sfdistrictattorney.org/restorative-justice

Ellison, J., & Partridge, J. A. (2012). Relationships between shame-coping, fear of failure, and perfectionism in college athletes. *Journal of Sport Behavior*, *35*(1).

Elliott, L. (2018). A Geometry of its own: restorative justice, relationships and community in democracy. In *Cutting the Edge* (pp. 153-169). Routledge.

Hung, M. (2015). Talking circles promote equitable discourse. *Mathematics Teacher*, *109*(4), 256-260.

Igwe, F. (2018). *Healing Circles: Using a Restorative Justice Practice to Address Identity Reformation amongst Black Men Post Incarceration* (Doctoral dissertation, Indiana University).

Johnstone, G. (2020). The standardization of restorative justice. In *Rights and restoration within youth justice*.

Kim, W. C., & Mauborgne, R. A. (2003, January). Fair process: Managing in the knowledge economy. *Harvard Business Review*, 127-136.

Kirkwood, S., & Hamad, R. (2019). Restorative justice informed criminal justice social work and probation services. *Probation Journal*, *66*(4), 398-415.

Kumar, R., Karabenick, S. A., Warnke, J. H., Hany, S., & Seay,

N. (2019). Culturally Inclusive and Responsive Curricular Learning Environments (CIRCLEs): An exploratory sequential mixed-methods approach. *Contemporary Educational Psychology, 57,* 87-105.

Marshall, C. D. (2020). Restorative justice. In *Religion Matters* (pp. 101-117). Springer, Singapore.

McCold, P. (2001). Primary restorative justice practices. *Restorative Justice for Juveniles, Hart Publishing, Oxford,* 41-58.

McCold, P., & Wachtel, T. (2003, August). *In pursuit of paradigm: A theory of restorative justice.* Paper presented at the XIII World Congress of Criminology, Rio de Janeiro, Brazil.

Mehl-Madrona, L., & Mainguy, B. (2014). Introducing healing circles and talking circles into primary care. *The Permanente Journal, 18*(2), 4.

Miner, K. (2010, January 16). How to run a meeting like a Restorative Justice Talking Circle. Retrieved April 18, 2020, from http://www.circle-space.org/2010/01/18/how-to-run-a-meeting-like-a-restorative-justice-talking-circle/

Nathanson, D. (1997). From empathy to community. *Annual of Psychoanalysis, 25,* 125-143.

Ortiz, M. (2019). *Restorative Justice in the Criminal Justice System: A Content Analysis.* California State University, Long Beach.

Percival, C. S. (2003). *Testing Braithwaite's theory of reintegrative shaming through data on the circle sentencing program in the Yukon* (Doctoral dissertation, University of Hawaii at Manoa).

Restorative Justice. (n.d.). Retrieved April 18, 2020, from https://www.uky.edu/studentconduct/restorative-justice

Rogers, R., & Miller, H. V. (2018). Restorative justice. *The Handbook of Social Control,* 167-180.

Schiff, M. (2018). Can restorative justice disrupt the 'school-to-prison pipeline?'. *Contemporary Justice Review, 21*(2), 121-139.

Simpson, K. (2016, October 13). Denver woman feels the power of restorative justice after son murdered. Retrieved April 18, 2020, from https://www.denverpost.com/2012/07/09/denver-woman-feels-the-power-of-restorative-justice-after-son-murdered/

Sitemap, Rjc, & Restorative Justice Council. (n.d.). Restorative Justice Council: Promoting quality restorative practice for everyone. Retrieved April 18, 2020, from https://restorativejustice.org.uk/

Talking Piece. (n.d.). Retrieved April 18, 2020, from https://theidealisticeducator.wordpress.com/tag/talking-piece/

Tomkins, S. (1987). Shame. In D.L. Nathanson (Ed.). *The many faces of shame* (pp. 133-161). New York, NY: Norton.

Wilson, C. (2018). A history of the development of circles of support and accountability. In *Sexual crime and circles of support and accountability* (pp. 1-23). Palgrave Macmillan, Cham.

Winters, A., & America, N. (2014). Using Talking Circles in the classroom. *Heartland Community College, 1*.

Umbreit, M. S., & Greenwood, J. (2000, April). Guidelines for victim-sensitive victim-offender mediation: Restorative justice through dialogue. Washington, DC: U.S. Department of Justice, Office for Victims of Crime.

ABOUT THE AUTHOR

Joe Barnett

Joe is an avid reader and researcher in the field of criminal justice. His career of over 20 years in the criminal justice field has brought him unparalleled experience in the areas of fraud, employee theft, lie detection, and anti-terrorism. Joe has worked in both the public and private sector as a criminal justice specialist where he has earned awards and spoke to audiences around the country. During this time, Joe has earned a B.S of Criminal Justice from  The Ohio University and a M.S from The University of Cincinnati. Joe continues to work in the field of criminal justice and adds to the body of research in which it encompasses.

BOOKS BY THIS AUTHOR

Racial Profiling In A Post 9/11 Society

After the tragic events of September 11, 2001, does racial profiling make us safer? Some people would say that targeting certain groups, or ethnicities, will keep the threat of terrorism low. Is there evidence that can support this claim? Since 9/11, race and racial profiling has been a very hot topic.